HANDBOOK

OF THE

FIJIAN

LANGUAGE,

BY THE

REV. WILLIAM MOORE.

MDCCCXCIII.

G. L. GRIFFITHS, PRINTER, SUVA, FIJI.

SUVA, FIJI.
G. L. Griffiths, Printer.
1898.

PREFACE.

The first edition of this little Book owed its appearance to a request from H.B.M. Consul (Captain H. M. Jones, V.C.,) that I should prepare a small "HANDBOOK FOR IMMIGRANTS, MORE SIMPLE AND LESS EXPENSIVE THAN OUR PRESENT BOOKS." In sending out the second edition, I may say that I make no pretensions to originality, except in *plan*. Although I have made preparations for greatly enlarging and otherwise improving this little "Key," yet, in deference to the opinion of others, it is now reprinted with only some few corrections and additions, to meet a pressing want.

WM. MOORE.

Levuka, Ovalau, 1881.

CONTENTS.

		PAGE
	PREFACE	3
1.	THE KEY TO THE LANGUAGE	5
2.	THE ALPHABET	6
3.	THE ARTICLES...	6
4.	THE NOUNS	7
5.	ADJECTIVES	8
6.	NUMERALS	9
7.	PRONOUNS	9
8.	VERBS	11
9.	ADVERBS	13
10.	PREPOSITIONS	13
11.	CONJUNCTION	13
12.	INTERJECTIONS	13
13.	USEFUL WORDS TO BE LEARNT FIRST ...	13
14.	USEFUL SENTENCES ON LANDING ...	14
15.	HOUSEHOLD WORDS, &c.	15
16.	WORDS FOR GARDEN, PLANTATION, &c.	19
17.	WORDS FOR BOATING AND CANOES ...	21
18.	WORDS FOR PARTS OF THE HUMAN BODY	22
19.	WORDS FOR RELALIONSHIP	24
20.	WORDS FOR NATURALIST AND BOTANIST	25
21.	WORDS REQUIRING CARE WITH AI ...	28
22.	A SHORT VOCABULARY	33

THE KEY

TO THE

FIJIAN LANGUAGE.

1.—KEY.

"A cava oqo?" What's this?

You have the Key wherewith to open your way into the language in the above sentence, pronounced in English "Ah thava ongo?" If you can procure a native, do so by all means, and, placing the Alphabet before you, ply him with your Key "A cava oqo?" until you get the proper sounds. Be careful of B, C, D, G, Q, and do not proceed until you have mastered your Alphabet. This done, begin at once to note down everything around you. Pointing to a stone, use your Key, "A cava oqo?" The answer will be, "A vatu." "Oqo," this. "Oqori," that (near). "Ko ya," that (distant.) Keep this in mind, and will make your Key more definite and successful.

2. ALPHABET.

Form.	Name.	Power.
a	a	as *a* in father, alas
b	mba	as *mb* in member, number
c	tha	as *th* in that, this; not as in thick
d	nda	as *nd* in end, hand
e	a	as *a* in fate, hate
f	fa	as *f* in English, used in introduced words
g	nga	as *ng* in sing, rang
i	e	as *e* in me, or *i* in machine
j	ja	as *j* in English, in introduced words
k	ka	as *k* in English
l	la	as *l* in English
m	ma	as *m* in English
n	na	as *n* in English
o	o	as *o* in mote note
p	pa	as *p* in English, in introduced words
q	ngga	as *ngg* in younger, stronger, or *nk* in bank
r	ra	rather harder than *r* in English
s	sa	as *s* in English
t	ta	nearly same as *t* in English
u	oo	as *oo* in wood, or *u* in full
v	va	as *v* in English
w	wa	as *w* in English
y	ya	as *y* when a consonant in English

N.B.—At Lau they substitute *j* for *t*; as, *t*iko is *j*iko, &c.
At Cakaudrovi they reject k; as, la*k*o is la'o, &c.

3.—ARTICLES.

The ARTICLES are as follows:—

Ko and Na.—These take different forms; as, ko and o, koi and oi, na and a, nai and ai. Ko and o, koi and oi are used only before

(1.) Names of persons; as, Ko or O Joni.
(2.) Names of officials; as Ko or O Roko Tui Bau.
(3.) Names of places; as, Ko or O Bau.

A, na, ai, nai, are the same Articles; but some words will take ai or nai only. The Articles are not effected by number.

As a general rule, a and ai are used at the *beginning* of a sentence, and na and nai in the *middle*; as,

A tamata maivei na tamata ko ya?
A man—whence, the man that?
Ai sele cava nai sele oqo?
A knife, what the knife this?

Care is needed in the use of the *i*.

Examples.

A matau, an axe.	Ai matau, the right hand.
A matai, a carpenter.	Ai matai, the first.
A sele, a cut pig.	Ai sele, a knife.
A yau, to carry.	Ai yau, riches, property, &c.

(See list towards end of book.)

4.—NOUNS.

(1.) DERIVATION.

(For Derivations and peculiarities, see Grammar, p. 9.)

All adjectives are used as abstract nouns, as,

Vinaka, good, goodness.
Ca, bad, badness.

Almost all nouns that express actions, agents, and instruments, are derived from verbs.

The simple form of the verb is used as a noun; or, by prefixing vei dau, and dauvei; or, by compounding the verbs, nouns may be formed.

Examples.

A butako, a thief.	Butako, to steal.
A veicati, enmity.	Cata, to hate.
A daubutako, a thief.	Butako, to steal.
A dauveibeitaki, an accuser.	Beitaka, to accuse.
A dau-ni-vucu, a poet.	Vucu, to sing, &c.

(2.) GENDER.

Mas.	Fem.
A tagane, a male.	A ewa, a female.
A tama-na, a father.	A tina-na, a mother.
A turaga, a chief.	A marama, a lady.
A tuka-na, a grandfather.	A bui, a grandmother.
A tui, a king.	A yadi or adi, a queen.
A sarn, a boar.	A tinatina, a sow.
Ai talaki, a man-servant.	A vada, a maid-servant.
Ratu, Sir.	Adi, Madam.
Tamatama, a father (of inferior animals.)	Tinatina, mother (of inferior animals.)

Common Gender.

A luve-na, a son or daughter.
A wati-na, a husband or wife.
A tamata, mankind.

All genders are formed by *tagane* or *alewa*, after the noun; as,

A gone tagane, a boy.	A gone alewa, a girl.
A toa tagane, a cock.	A toa alewa, a hen.
A ga tagane, a drake.	A ga alewa, a duck.

(3.) NUMBER.

By prefixing one of the *numerals*, or *vei*, or a *personal pronoun*, you form the singular, dual, and plural.

Example.

Dua: Definite sign, singular; as,

E dua na tamata, a man, a *certain* man.

Vei, with nouns, is a plural and collective sign. It *cannot* be used with *all* nouns, and it is difficult to give a general rule. Do not use it before things with *animal life*.

Pronouns, Personal.

Singular—O koya na tamata, the man; or, he the man.
Dual—Oi rau na tamata, the two men; or, they the two men.
Plural—O ira na tamata, the men; or, they the men.

(4.) CASE.

(For definite and indefinite, see Grammar, p. 16)

Declension. Singular.

Nom.—O, or ko koya na tamata. He the man.	the man.
Poss.—A nona na tamata. His the man.	the man's.
Obj.—Koya na tamata. Him the man.	the man.
Voc.—O iko na tamata. You the man.	man.

Or, the three numbers at one view; as,

Singular.	*Dual.*	*Plural.*
Nom.—O koya na tamata.	Oi rau na tamata.	O ira na tamata.
Poss.—A nona na tamata.	A nodrau na tamata.	A nodra na tamata.
Obj.—Koya na tamata.	Rau na tamata.	Kemudou na tamata.
Voc.—O iko na tamata.	Oi Kemudrau na tamata.	Oi kemudou na tamata.

N.B.—For the use of nena, kena, mena, and their plurals, see Grammar, p. 17.

5.—ADJECTIVES.

(On *Derivatives*, &c., see Grammar, p. 20.)

Singular.	*Plural.*
A tamata levu.	A tamata lelevu.
A man great.	Men great.
A ka lekaleka.	A ka leleka.
A thing short.	Things short.

Degrees of Comparison.

We have no regular form in the adjective itself to express comparison. It is formed by the *addition of a word*, or by *contrast;* as,

Lailai sobu.   Levu cake.
   Little below; (less.)   Great above; (greater.)

When several things are together, then—

A cava na ka e vinaka?
Which the thing (is) good? *Or*,
Which is *the* good thing—the best.

Good.	Better.	Best.
Vinaka.	Vinaka cake.	Vinaka sara.

A tamata *vinaka*, a good man.
A tamata vinaka cake, a better man.
A tamata vinaka sara, the good or best man.
A tamata vinaka taudua (or daudua), the incomparable man.

6.—NUMERALS.

Dua, 1; Rua, 2; Tolu, 3; Va, 4; Lima, 5; Ono, 6; Vitu, 7; Walu, 8; Ciwa, 9; O, 0.

Kena caca (e dua)	1 One
Tini	10 Ten
Tini ka dua—Ten and One, &c.	11 Eleven
Ruasagavulu	20 Twenty
Ruasagavulu kadua, &c.	21 &c.
Tolusagavulu	30
Tolusagavulu kadua, &c.	31
Vasagavulu, &c., &c.	40
Limasagavulu	50
Drau	100
E dua na drau ka dua	101
Udolu	1,000
Oba	10,000
Vetelei	100,000
Petele	1,000,000
Wakaniniu	10,000,000
Matininuku	100,000,000

They are used of both gender and numbers.

(2.) ORDINALS.
Ai Matai, 1st, Ai karua, 2nd; Ai katolu, 3rd; &c.

(3) DISTRIBUTIVES.
Yadua, one each. Yarua, two each, &c.

(4) COLLECTIVES.
Duadua, one only. Ruarua, both, &c.

(5) ADVERBS OF TIME.
Vakadua, once. Vakarua, twice, &c.

7.—PRONOUNS.

We believe there are four numbers, but do not trouble the beginner with four.

(1.) PERSONAL.

Singular.	Dual.	Plural.
Au, I.	Kedaru, we two.	Keda & Kedatou, we.
Iko, thou.	Kemudrau, you two.	Kemudou, you.
Koya, he.	Koirau, they two.	Ko ira, them, they.

(2.) POSSESSIVE.

A noqu, my, mine.	A nodaru, (of two) ours, our.	A noda, our, ours.
A nomu, thy, thine.	A nomudrau (of two) yours, you.	A nomudou, you, yours.
A nona, his, hers.	A nodrau (of two) they, theirs.	A nodra, theirs.

HANDBOOK OF

(3.) RELATIVE.

1. Personal pronouns are used as *relative*.

Example.

A cava ena cakava ko koya vei ira, *era* sa cati koya?
What will he do to them *who* hate him.

2. *Possessive* pronouns are also used as *relative*.

Example.

O cei na turaga oqo, a *nona* vosa ko sa kauta mai?
Who is the chief *whose* commands you bring?

3. *Demonstrative* pronouns are also used as *relative*.
Viz.—O ya, ko ya, a ya, oqo, oqori.

Example.

Evei na tamata *ko ya*, ka kauta mai oqo?
Where is the man who brought this?

4. The *compound* pronoun is used as a *relative*.

Example.

A tamata ka'u a vosa *vua* me tara noqu vale. The man to *whom* I spoke to build my house.

A tamata keirau a tiko *kaya*.
The man with *whom* I dwell.

5. *Kina* may be used to both *persons* and *things*.

Example.

A tamata ka'u a vosa kina.
The man *to* (of) *whom* I spoke.
A ka kau a vosa *kina*.
The things of which I spoke.

Kina is used for—to whom, by whom, for whom, and in whom: to which, by which, for which, and in which.

4. INTERROGATIVE PRONOUNS.

There are two, viz.—O cei, or ko cei, *who*, of persons, and a cava, *what*, of things. They are used of both gender and numbers.

5. REFLECTIVE PRONOUNS.

Examples.

Au sa lako koi au. I go myself.
O sa lako ko iko, se segai? Do you go *yourself* or not?
Au sa yaviti au. I strike myself.

6. DEMONSTRATIVE PRONOUNS.

Examples.

This, these.
Oqo—Singular or plural.
O koya oqo—Singular.
O ira oqo—Plural.

That, those.
Oqori—Singular or plural.
O koya oqori—Singular.
O ira oqori—Plural.
O ya—Generally singular.
O koya ko ya—Singular.

THE FIJIAN LANGUAGE.

8.—VERBS.

These will require a careful study of Hazlewood's Grammar. We can only give you an idea of the peculiarities of the verb. The classification adopted is of importance, viz,—1. Intransitive; 2. Active transitive; 3. Neuter intransitive, and Transitive. These will require time and study to master. We refer you to the Grammar.

We give the following as examples of the uses of the verbal signs of tense, and of the different forms of pronouns used before moods:—

INDICATIVE MOOD.

Present tense.

Per.   *Singular.*
1. Au sa lako, I go.
2. Ko sa lako, you go.
3. Sa lako ko koya, he goes.

Per.   *Dual.*
1. incl. Edaru sa lako, we two go.
    excl. Keirau sa lako, we two go.
2. Kemudrau sa lako, you two go.
3. Erau sa lako, they two go.

Triad, or few.
1. incl. Edatou sa lako, we three go.
    excl. Keitou sa lako, we three go.
2. Kemudou sa lako, you three go.
3. Eratou sa lako, they three go.

Plural.
1. incl. Eda sa lako, we go.
    excl. Keimami sa lako, we go.
2. Kemuni sa lako, you go.
3. Era sa lako, they go.

N.B.—Substitute *a* for *sa* in the *past*, and *na* for *sa* in the *future*.

IMPERATIVE MOOD.

Singular.
1. Me'u lako, let me go.
2. Mo lako, go you.
3. Me lako ko koya, let him go.

Dual.
1. incl. Daru lako, let us two go.
    excl. Me keirau lako, let us two go.
2. Drau lako go you two.
3. Me rau lako, let them two go.

Triad, or few.
1. incl. Tou lako, let us three go.
    excl. Me keitou lako, let us three go.
2. Dou lako, go you.
3. Me ratou lako, let them go.

Plural.
1. incl. Me da lako, let us go.
    excl. Me keimami lako, let us go.
2. Mo ni lako, go you.
3. Me ra lako, let them go.

SUBJUNCTIVE MOOD.

This mood is indicated by the conjunction ME, *that*, or *to the end of that*.

Let it be observed that the difference is in the *signs* and *pronouns*, and not in the verb.

Singular.

1. Sa kaya me'u lako, (he) says that I am to go.
2. Sa kaya me lako, (he) says that you are to go.
3. Sa kaya me lako ko koya, (he) says that he is to go.

Dual.

1. incl. Sa kaya me daru lako, (he) says that we two are to go.
    excl. Sa kaya me keirau lako, (he) says that we two are to go.
2. Sa kaya mo drau lako, (he) says that you two are to go.
3. Sa kaya me rau lako, (he) says that they two are to go.

Triad.

1. incl. Sa kaya me datou lako, (he) says that we are to go.
   excl. Sa kaya me keitou lako, (he) says that we are to go.
2. Sa kaya me kemudou lako, (he) says that you are to go.
3. Sa kaya me ratou lako, (he) says that they are to go.

Plural.

1. incl. Sa kaya me da lako, (he) says that we are to go.
   excl. Sa kaya me keimami lako, (he) says that we are to go.
2. Sa kaya mo ni lako, (he) says that ye are to go.
3. Sa kaya me ra lako, (he) says that they are to go.

CONDITIONAL MOOD.

It will be observed that a longer form of several pronouns is used after kevaka, if, than that which is used in the imperative and subjunctive moods; as, kevaka eda, not kevaka da, which renders it necessary to consider the conditional mood separately.

Singular.

1. Kevaka k'au sa lako, if I go.
2. Kevaka ko sa lako, if you go.
3. Kevaka sa lako ko koya, if he goes.

Dual.

1. incl. Kevaka edaru sa lako, if we two go.
   excl. Kevaka keirau sa lako, if we two go.
2. Kevaka drau sa lako, if you two go.
3. Kevaka erau sa lako, if they two go.

Triad, or few.

1. incl. Kevaka edatou sa lako, if we go.
   excl. Kevaka keitou sa lako, if we go.
2. Kevaka dou sa lako, if you go.
3. Kevaka eratou sa lako, if you go.

Plural.

1. incl. Kevaka eda sa lako, if we go.
   excl. Kevaka keimami sa lako, if we go.
2. Kevaka kemuni sa lako, if ye go.
3. Kevaka era sa lako, if they go.

Here edaru, edatou, eda, eran, eratou, era, are used as well as when they begin a sentence, which is not the case in the imperative or subjunctive moods.

INFINITIVE MOOD.

Me lako, to go.

PARTICIPLES.

They have the same form as the verb, except that sometimes an auxiliary verb is added to make them more definite; as, Dou sa lako kivei? Where are you going? Or, Dou sa lako *tiko* kivei? Where are you *now* going?

9.—ADVERBS.

1. Of *manner*. Formed by prefixing *vaka*; as, vaka ca, badly.
2. Of *time*. Edaidai, to-day. Edaidai oqo, now.
3. Of *place*. Eke, ekaka, here; kikea, kikeri, maikea, there, &c.
4. Of *affirmation*. Io, yes; segai, no, not; tawa, not; e lasu, false, not so; e tabu, it is unlawful, &c.

10.—PREPOSITIONS.

There are but three, viz,—E or i, in; ki, to; mai, from.

Examples.

Au sa tiko e Viti, I am *in* Fiji.
Kauti au ki Bau, take me *to* Bau.
Kau a tiko mai Bau, I have come *from* Bau.

Few prepositions are needed, as the verbal terminations answer as such.

11.—CONJUNCTIONS.

These are ka, kai, and kei, which connect verbs, or adjectives, and adverbs.
Kei connects nouns and pronouns.
Kai is only used when the noun requires *i* prefixed.
Se, or, whether; sa lako se segai, gone or not.
Ke, kevaka, if; ga, only; ia ka, but; ia, yea.
De, lest, perhaps; ni, for, because or since.
O koya, kina, a ka oqo, therefore.

12.—INTERJECTIONS.

Almost innumerable. Drasa, &c. See Grammar, p. 60.

13.—A PAGE OF USEFUL WORDS TO BE LEARNT FIRST.

Comet	Kalokalo Vakabuina, or ai tata	Dearth	Dausiga
		Hot	Katakata
World	Vuravura	Rock	Vatu
Heaven	Lomalagi	Island	Yanuyanu
Sun	Siga	Current	Kui
Moon	Vula	Land	Vanua
Stars	Kalokalo	Earth	Qele
Eclipse of sun	Buto-leka	Food	Kakana
Do. of moon	Mate-ni-vula	Town	Koro
Clouds	O, or ou	Boat	Velovelo
Rain	Uca	Tree	Kau
Wind	Cagi	Wood	Veikau
Storm	Cagi kaukauwa	Ship	Waqa-vanua
Hurricane	Cagi ravu, cava	Canoe	Waqa
Flood	Waluvu and Naluvu	Stone	Vatu
		Shells	Vivili

Cold	Liliwa	Fowls	Toa
Cool	Mudremudre	Birds	Manumanu vuka
Air	Mudre	Ducks	Ga
Rainbow	Drodrolagi	Turtle	Ika bula
Light	Rarama	Pig	Vuaka
Day	Siga	Chief	Turaga, tui
Night	Bogi	Lady	Marama
Winter	Vula i liliwa	Yam	Uvi
Summer	Vula i katakata	Potato	Kawai
East	Matanisiga, tokalau	Hungry	Viakana
		Thirsty	Viagunu
West	Ra	Sleep	Moce, via moce
North	Vualiku	Weary	Oca
South	Ceva	House	Vale
Mountain	Ulunivanua	Man	Tamata
Cape	Ucuna	Woman	Alewa
Isthmus	Yarabale	Turkey	Pipi, or taki
Ridge	Babana	Child	Gone
Lake	Waimate	Girl	Gone alewa
Coast	Baravi	Boy	Gone tagane
Gulf	Toba titobu	Father	Tama-qu, na, &c.
Bay	Toba	Mother	Tina-qu, na, &c.
Passage	Daveta	Brother	Taci-qu, na, &c.
Channel	Kena wai	Sister	Gane-qu, na, &c.
Reef	Cakau	Husband	Wati-qu, na, &c.
Shoal	Matia	Wife	Wati-qu, na, &c.
Sunken rock	Yamoto	Son	Luve-qu tagane
Sea	Wasawasa	Daughter	Luve-qu alewa
River	Uciwai	Axe	Matau
Creek	Waidrodro	Knife	Ai sele
Water	Wai		

14.—USEFUL SENTENCES ON LANDING.

Who is the chief here ? Ko cei na turaga eke ?
Where is the town ? E vei na koro ?
Where is the chief ? E vei na turaga ?
What is your name ? O cei na yacamu ?
Where is your house ? Sai vei na nomu vale ?
Come with me. Me daru lako vata.
I want to eat. Au sa via kana.
I want to drink. Au sa via gunu.
I want to sleep. Au sa via moce.
Bring some wood. Kauta mai na buka.
Bring some fire. Kauti mai na buka waqa.
Bring some drinking water. Kauta mai na wai ni gunu.
Bring some drinking-nuts. Kauta mai na niu bu.
Bring some oranges. Kauta mai na moli.
Bring some bananas. Kauta mai eso na vudi.
What is the price of eggs? A cava nai voli ni yaloka?
What is the price of fowls ? A cava nai voli ni toa.
What is the price of fish ? A cava nai voli ni ika?

How is this done? Sa caka vakaevei oqo?
Is this the way to Rewa? Oqo no saia ki Rewa?
Is it far to Rewa? Sa yawa ki Rewa?
I want some shells. Au sa via rawata na vivili.
Have you any oil? Sa sa na waiwai vei iko?
What is the price of this? A cava na kenai voli?
It is not worth that. Sa sega ni rauta.
I will give you this. Au na solia oqo vei iko.
I don't want to buy. Au sa sega ni via volla.
Come another day. Lako mai e dua tale na siga.
Do this to-day? Me rawa edaidai ga.
Have you a canoe? Sa dua na nomu waqa?
Take me to Bau. Kauti au ki Bau.
Bring me back to-morrow. Kauti au tale e na sabogibogi.
What is the price of this mat? A cava nai voli ni ibi oqo?
Bring me a pig. Kauta mai e dua na vuaka.
Have you a native pudding? Sa dua na vakalolo?
Where is the Native Church? Sai vei na vale ni lotu?
Have you an English Church? Sa dua na vale ni lotu vaka-
 [papalagi?
Are they fighting in this Town? Sai valu na koro oqo?
Land my goods. Me sobu mai na noqu ka.
Put them in this house. Me yau ki na vale oqo.
Don't get them wet. Me kakua ni suasua.
Be quick back. Mo kusa tale mai.
This is for you. Sa nomu oqo.
Can I stay with you? Ka'u tiko rawa eke?
Don't you get drunk. Kakua ni ko mateni.
Let us be friends, Me daru veiwekani.

15.—HOUSEHOLD WORDS.

1. Dining Room.

House	Vale	Dish	Dari
Dining room	Vale ni kana	Cup and saucer	Bilo ni ti
Table	Lalakai, tepeli	Jug	Juki
Table cover	Ai ubi ni lalakai	Tumbler	Bilo iloilo
Sofa	Ai davodavo	Plate	Dari
Chair	Ai tikotiko	Milk	Sucu
Sideboard	Kopati	Fowls	Toa
Window	Ai iloilo	Pudding	Purini
Door	Katuba	Arrowroot	Yabia
Mat	Ibi	Cork	Ai sogo
Looking-glass	Ai iloilo	Candle	Cina uro
Lamp	A cina	Bread	Madrai
Knife	Ai sele	Salt	Masima
Fork	Ai cula	Pepper	Pepa, boro
Spoon	Ai taki	Cruet stand	Tutu ni tavaya
Steel	A vagata ni sele	Bell	Lali [kau
Tea tray	Dari ni bilo ni ti	Butter	Uro ni bulumo-
Window curtain	Sulu ni iloilo	Pork	Vuaka
Tea	Ti, Waikatakata	Eggs	Yaloka

HANDBOOK OF

Coffee	Kofi	Rice	Raisi
Cheese	Uro kaukauwa ni bulumokau	Decanter	Tavaya ni yaqona

Be quick. Kusarawa; or, Mo kusarawa.
Prepare the food. Vakarautaka na kakana.
Bring in the food. Kauta mai na kakana.
Is the food cooked? Sa buta na kanana, sa segai?
Bring a chair. Kauta mai nai tikotiko.
Bring a knife. Kauta mai nai sele.
Bring a light. Kauta mai na cina.
Clean the knives. Masia nai sele.
Wash the plates, &c. Derea na bilo.
Dust the house. Qusia na vale.
Sweep the house. Taviraka na vale.
Wipe this. Qusia oqo.
Shut the door. Sogota na katuba.
Open the door. Dolava na katuba.
Put up the curtains. Viviga nai sulu ni iloilo.
Change the plates. Vuki na dari.
Wipe the knives. Qusia nai sele.
Wash the tumblers. Derea na bilo iloilo.
Bring some bananas. Kauta mai na vudi eso.
Bring some water. Kauta mai na wai ni gunu.
Draw the cork. Me cavu nai sogo.
Clear away the plates. Kauta tani na dari.

2. BED ROOM. *(Vale ni moce.)*

Bedstead	Ai davodavo	Mat	Ibi
Bed	Ai mocemoce	Hair-oil	Ai lumu
Blanket	Sulu vutikana	Clean	Savasava
Sheet	Ai tutuvi	Dirty	Qeleqelea
Pillow	Ai lokoloko	Filthy	Velavela
Curtain	Taunamu	Sleep	Moce
Counterpane	Ai ubi ni moce-	Rise	Yadra
Chamber	A po [moce	Rise early	Yadra taudonu
Drawers	A toroa	Damp	Suasua
Looking-glass	Ai iloilo	Come	Lako mai
Washstand	Ai tutu ni tavoi	Go	Lako yani
Wash basin	Ai vuluvulu	Sufficient	Sa levu
Jug	Juki	To comb	Serutaka
Soap	A vuso, or sovu	Scissors	Ai koti
Comb	Ai seru	Razor	Ai toroi
Tooth brush	Ai masi ni bati	Go to sleep	Sa laki moce
Water, cold	Wai liliwa	Clean water	Wai savasava
Water, hot	Wai katakata	Open the box	Dolava na rubu
Bath	Wai ni sili	Rub the chairs	Masia nai tikotiko
Towel	Ai tavoi	Be quick	Tatama, kusa
Box	Rubu	Good morning	Sa yadra
Chair	Ai tikotiko		

Make the bed. Cakava nai mocemoce
Prepare the room. Vakarautaka na vale.

Is the room ready?   Sa vakarau oti na vale?
Are the sheets dry?   Sa mamaca nai tutuvi?
Bring the blanket.   Kauta mai nai sulu vutikana.
Have you a pillow?   Sa dua na lokoloko vei iko?
Put the curtains down.   Me lutu na taunamu.
Put the curtains up.   Me cere na taunamu.
Take the curtains off.   Me luva na taunamu.
Wash the sheets.   Me sava nai tutuvi.
Put clean towels.   Me tu nai tavoi savasava.
Empty the chamber.   Derea na po.
Move the bed here.   Me vuki nai mocemoce kike.
Be quick.   Mo kusarawa.
Bring some water.   Kauta mai eso na wai.
Prepare the bath.   Vakarautaka nai silisili.
Sweep the room.   Taviraka na vale.
Sun the mats.   Sigana na ibi.
Bring some hot water.   Kauta mai na wai katakata.
Take out all the things.   Kauta kece ki tuba.
Scrub the floor.   Masia na papa.
Dust the furniture.   Qusia nai yaya ni vale.

3. Kitchen and Cooking.

Kitchen	Vale ni kuro	Beef	Bulumokau
Fire	Buka, or buka-waqa	Mutton	Sipi
		Pork, pig	Vuaka
Firewood	Buka	Fowls	Toa
Fireplace	Matadravu	Ducks	Ga
Coals	Qilaiso	Fish	Ika
Kettle	Tikeri	Cooked	Sabuta
Pot	Kuro	Underdone	Sa droka
Fry-pan	Tavuteki	Burnt	Sa qesa
Gridiron	Ai tavutavu	Eggs	Yaloka
Oven	Oveni, or lovo	Boil	Me riri
Saucepan	Sosepani	To fry	Tavuteki
Hot	Katakata	Bake	Me vavi
Boil	Kere	Roast	Tavuna
Hot water	Wai katakata	Grill	Tavuna
Tea	Wai katakata	Pluck, fowl, &c.	Vutia
Soup	Wai buta	Kill, pig, &c.	Vakamatea
Fowl soup	Wai ni toa.	To salt	Vakamasima-taka
Fish soup	Wai ni ika		
Potatoes	Kawai	To soak	Tanu e wai
Yams	Uvi	Stuff, season	Vakasaso
Pumpkin	Titimo	Onion	Varasa
Greens	Rourou	Orange, Lemon	Moli

Is the water ready?   Sa vakarau oti na wai?
Is the pork done?   Sa buta na vuaka?
Are the eggs cooked?   Sa buta na yaloka?
Make a good fire.   Me vakalevu na buka.
Have a slow fire.   Me vakalailai na buka.
Have plenty of hot water.   Me vakalevu na wai katakata.

Put this in hot water. Me tu oqo e na wai katakata.
Put this in cold water. Me tu oqo e na wai liliwa.
Keep this warm. Me katakata tu oqo.
Don't burn this. Kakua ni qesa oqo.
This is spoiled. Sa ca sara oqo.
This is burnt. Sa qesa oqo.
This is done nicely. Sa buta vinaka oqo.
You are a careless fellow. Sa tamata wele ko iko.
You are a good fellow. Sa tamata vinaka ko iko.
Do it like this. Mo kitaka vaka oqo.
Get some greens. Me rawa eso na rourou.
Boil some bananas. Me riri eso na vudi.
Bake some bananas. Me vavi eso na vudi.
Roast some bananas. Me tavu eso na vudi.
Toast some bread. Me tavu eso na madrai.
Cover up the fire. Me bulu na buka.
Don't be long. Kakua ni dede.

(4.) Nursery and Laundry.

Nurse	Meme	Carry on back	Vava
Baby	Gone	Button	Bulukau
Milk	Sucu	Needle	Cula
Feed	Vakania	Thread	Wa
Wash	Vakasilima	Scissors	Ai koti
Dress	Vakasuluma	To sew	Culacula
Frock	Ai curucuru	To wash face	Tavoi
Petticoat	A liku	To wash clothes	Sava
Shirt	Sulu e loma	To wash, or bathe	Sisili
Shoes	Ai vava	To wash chamber	Vuya
Socks	Sulu ni yava	Soap	Vuso
Gloves	Sulu ni liga	Iron, flat	Vatu ni sulu
Hat or bonnet	Ai sala	Blue	Wai loaloa
Belt	Ai vakamau	Hooks and eyes	Bulukau veve
Necklace	Ai taubi	Bodkin	Ai dara ni wa
Coat	A koti	Mangle	Ai qaqi ni sulu
Necktie	Ai taubi	Starch	Yabia
Trousers	Sulu dara	Fold	Lobia
Handkerchief	Ai tavoi	Wring	Loba
Flannel	Sulu katakata	Sun	Sigana
Umbrella	Ai vakaruru	Cry	Tagi
To nurse	Roqo	Cough	Vu

Bring the baby here. Kauta mai kike na gone.
Feed the baby at once. Vakania sara oqo na gone.
Wash and dress the baby. Me sili ka vakaisulu na gone.
Milk the goat for baby. Lobaka na me, mena na gone.
Mend the clothes. Me cula nai sulu.
Stitch this along here. Me cula lesu oqo.
Hem this to-day. Me cula lobi oqo edaidai.
Gather this. Me cula vakasosouruuru oqo.
Sew these together. Me cula vivi oqo.
Run this together. Me cula vata oqo.

Clean the children's boots. Masia nai vava ni gone.
Bring a clean towel. Kauta mai nai tavoi savasava.
Boil the clothes. Me saqa ni sulu.
Wash the clothes clean. Me savasava sara nai sulu.
Starch the shirts. Me vakayabia nai sulu.
Blue the clothes. Vakawailoaloataka nai sulu.
Sun the clothes. Me sigai nai sulu.
Keep out of the sun. Kakua ni lako ki na siga.
Don't leave the house. Kakua ni ko laiva na vale.
Make the arrowroot. Cakava na yabia.
Is the bed dry? Sa mamaca nai mocemoce?
Air the bed clothes. Sigana kece nai sulu ni mocemoce.
Don't be long away. Kakua ni ko dede.

16.—GARDEN, PLANTATION, &c.

Garden	Were	Lift	Lave, tabea
Axe	Matau	Help	Veivuke
Hatchet	Ai tivitivi	Tree	Kau
Knife	Ai sele	Root	Wakana
Spade	Ai sivi	Stem	Vuna
Rake		Branch	Tabana
Digging stick	Doko	Leaves	Drauna
Dig	Cuki	Bark	Kulina
Cut down	Ta sobu	Sap	Dra
Cut across	Ta musu	Green	Droka
Split	Ta sea	Dry	Mudu
Lop off	Ta masuka	Grass	Co, veico
Cut up	Tatalaka	Reeds	Gasau, veigasau
To fall, fell	Vakabalea	Brush	Veikaukau
Clear	Caramaka	Weeds	Veicoco
Weed	Wereca	Saw	Ai varo
Burn off	Visa	Flower	Sena
Plant	Tea	Pod	Kovu
Pick cotton	Sera	Berry	Vuana
Pluck fruit	Betea	Seed	Sorena
Drag	Yara	Basket	Tabi
Carry	Colata	Store	Lololo

Will you clear this? Mo wereca oqo, ne?
What will be the payment? A cava na kenai voli?
I will give you this. Au na solia oqo vei iko.
This is the payment. Oqo nai kenai voli.
This is for one month. Sa rauta na vula dua oqo.
You work one month. Mo cakacaka vula dua.
Bring a spade. Kauta mai nai sivi.
Dig all this. Cukiraka oqo kecega.
Take care of the axe. Koroya na matau.
Don't waste the seeds. Kakua ni yali na sorena.
Do it like this. Mo cakava vaka oqo.
Put this in the house. Me tu ki vale oqo.
Take this to John. Kauta oqo vei Joni.
Be here very early. Mo sou e na sabogibogi.

Cut this down and burn off. Ta oqo ka visa.

Clear off these weeds. Caramaka na veicoco oqo.

Put up this fence. Mo viria na bai oqo.

This is one hundred fathoms. Sa kata drau oqo.

Here is the payment, Oqo na kenai voli.

Dig it deep. Cukiraka vakatitobu.

Put out all the roots. Cavuta kece na wakana.

Follow this line. Muria nai vakarau oqo.

Plant at this distance. Me kena veiyawaki oqo.

What shall I give you to cut down and clear all this? A cava me'u solia vei iko mo taya sobu ka wereca oqo?

You fence in all this and I will give a gun. Mo viria kece na tikina oqo, kau na solia e dua na dakai.

What shall I give you to dig all this piece? A cava me'u solia vei iko, mo cukia na tikina kece oqo?

My friend, will you build me a good house? Noqui tau, mo tara e dua na noqu vale vinaka, ne?

I will give you these muskets for the house. K'au na solia vei iko na dakai oqo me ka ni vale.

I want these logs brought to this place. Me rawa na kau oqo ki na tikina oqo.

What shall I give you to plant all this piece? A cava me'u solia vei iko mo tea na tikina kece oqo?

Do not leave a single pod in the field. Kakua ni laiva e dua na kovu mai na were.

Do not play while you are at work; get on. Kakua na qito e na cakacaka, dou ia ga.

Bring me a hundred coffee plants and I will give this. Mo kauta mai e dua na drau na kofi, ia k'au na solia oqo.

Go and bring the food here and let all eat. La'ki kauta mai na kakana me ra kana kecega.

That will not do: it must be clean. E sega ni yaga oqo; me savasava ga.

Pick this row and then follow on in order. Vilica na tuatua oqo, ka qai uuria yadua oqo.

Collect these stones and build a fence with them. Soqona na vatu oqo ka viria kina na bai.

Let this tree stand for a shade and ornament. Me tu na kau oqo me vakaruru kei nai ukuuku.

Come very early in the morning and do this. Lako mai e na mataka caca sara ka kitaka oqo.

Chop off these limbs and put them together for burning. Ta musuka na tabana oqo ka soqona me visa.

Dry the cotton before you take it into the store. Sigana mada na vauvau ka qai kauta ki na lololo.

Get your breakfast first and then go and dig some yams. Katalau mada mo qai laki kilia eso na uvi.

Pick this cotton and take it into the house. Sera na vauvau oqo, ka mani kauta ki vale.

Pick up these ivi and then bake them for your food. Vilika na ivi oqo ka qai vavia me kemu.

When that is finished you can go home. Ni sa oti oqori, ko qai lako ki nomu vale.

Take this and go and purchase some yams. Kauta oqo ka laki volia eso na uvi.

Go and sharpen the axe and be quick back. La'ki vagata na matau ka mani kusa tale mai.

17.—BOATING AND CANOES.

Ship	Waqa vanua	Keel	Takele
Canoe	Waqa	Boards	Papa
Schooner	Sikuna	Nails	Ai vako
Steamer	Lacabuka	Paint	Ai boro
Boat	Velovelo	To paint	Boroya
Sail	Laca	To clean	Vuya
Rope	Dali	To scrub	Masia
Anchor	Ai kelikeli	Stem	Mua eliu
Rudder	Uli	Stern	Mua emuri
Oar	Ai voce	Gunwale	Batina
Rowlock	Ai vocevoce	Seats	Ai tikotiko
Sheets	Sila	Mast	Vana
Jib	Laca qasila	Mast (fore)	Vana eliu
Stays	Ai loba	Mast (main)	Vana e muri
Foresail	Laca eliu	Boom	Karikari levu
Mainsail	Laca e muri	Gaff	Karikari lailai
Keep away	Uli	Jibboom	Vana ni qasila
Luff { Windward	Tau	A pole	Doko
Luff { Windward, hard	Tau sara	Tide	Ua
		Ebb	Voka
Steady	Vinaka	Flow	Ua, or ua mai
Up sail	Vakarewa	High water	Ua levu
Down sail	Uru, Uruca	Low water	Sa matia
Pull away	Voce	East	Na tu e cako
Pole	Kara	West	Na ra
Paddle	Voce	North	Vualiku
Scull	Sua	South	Ceva
Slack sail	Vakarewa	East wind	Cagi na tu e cake
Sheet home	Sila sara	West wind	Cagi na ra
Shorten sail	Musu laca	North wind	Cagi a vualiku
Run (before wind)	Vui	South wind	Cagi a ceva
Fair wind	Cagi donu	Steer for	Muadonu ki
Foul wind	Cagi ca	Deep water	Wai titobu
Weather	Dreke	Shallow	Wai matia
Weather (good)	Drake vinaka	Scrape	Karia
Weather (bad)	Drake ca	Dry	Vakamamaca
Passage	Daveta	To bail	Nima
Reef	Cakau	Bailer	Ai nima
Shoal	Matia	Leak	Vakawai
Passage	Kena wai	To cork	Saubulu
Anchorage (good)	Kele vinaka	Cask, or keg	Saqa
Anchorage (bad)	Kele ca	Chain	Sinucodo
Splice	Sema	Compass	Kopasi
Let off sheet	Sorova	Watch (look out)	Rai toka
Painter (rope)	Ai noka	Be careful	Maroroya

Keep the boat up to the wind and be steady. Tau tiko ki na cagi, mo kakua ni yavala.

Up sail and let us get off early. Vakarewa me datou lako ni sa mataka.

Pull away, there's a storm coming. Voce sara sa dua na cagi levu sa lako mai.

Is there a passage in the reef or not? Sa dua na daveta e na cakau oqo se segai?

Take in sail and let us drift. Ura na laca me da ciri ga.

Shorten sail and be quick or we shall fill. Musu laca ka mani kusa de luvu na waqa.

Dry the sails or they will rot. Vakasiga na laca de mani vuca.

I want four men to pull me to Bau. Ka'u via rawata e va na tamata me vocetaki au ki Bau.

Get me some men that can pull well. Kauta mai eso na tamata e kila sara nai voce.

Can I pull to Rewa and back to-day? Kau voce rawa ki Rewa ka lesu tale edaidai?

Take care you do not break the oars. Mo raica vinaka de ramusu nai voce.

Keep the boat off the reef. Me kakua ni kasa e na cakau na velovelo.

William, go and beg some food for us. Wiliami, mo la'ki kerea eso na keda kakana.

Take some water and some yams in the boat. Kauta eso na wai kei na uvi e na velovelo.

The mast is broken; where shall we get another? Sa ramusu nai vana; ena kune maivei e dua tale?

Let John keep bailing; the boat leaks very badly. Me nima tiko ko Joni; sa vakawai sara na velovelo.

Pull away, boys; we shall get fast on the reef. Voce sara ragone; sa kasa na waqa e na cakau.

Be quick; see the breakers; the boat will be smashed. Kusa, raica na sese; sa na voca na velovelo.

The wind is strong; make the boat secure. Sa kaukauwa na cagi; kelia vinaka na waqa.

When we get to land look at the keel. Ni da sa yaco ki vanua, raica na takele.

Keep along inside the reef, in smooth water. Muria ga na wai cloma, e na wai mulumu.

Up with the jib, the foresail, and the mainsail. Vakarewa na laca qasila, na laca eliu, kei na laca e muri.

Let go the anchor, and stow the sails. Biu nai kelekele, ka mani vivi na laca.

Come early in the morning and let us go. Sou e na sabogibogi, me datou lako.

18.—PARTS OF THE HUMAN BODY.

Ulu-na	Head
Drau ni ulu	Hair
Yadre-na	Forehead
Vacu-na	Eyebrow
Mata	Eye
Vuluvulu ni mata	Eyelash
Ucu	Nose
Balu	Cheek
Kanavalavala	Temple
Babana	Cheek bone
Daliga	Ear
Gusu	Mouth
Bati	Teeth
Yame	Tongue
Yame-leka	
Gadro	Gums
Domo	Neck
Kesu	Back of the head
Coco	
Bogi ni gone	Soft part of head
Buturata	Crown of head
Ai vosatuisau	Third finger
Ai lokunimate	Little finger
Qeteqete ni liga	Palm of hand
Dakudaku ni liga	Back of hand
Ai sema	Under part of joints.
Sarisari	Sides of hands, body, &c.
Waqawaqa	Breast bone
Vureda	Lower edge of breast bone
Bati ni kete	Upper part of abdomen
Kete	Belly, abdomen
Ai vicovico	Navel
Dibi	Hip
Soga	Thigh
Kalova	Sides of thingh
Dolo siga	Front of thigh
Toki	Under the knee
Temu	Calf

THE FIJIAN LANGUAGE.

Vutuvutu ni tala	Shoulder	Ai vesi	Second finger
Kerikeri	Armpit	Qurulasawa]	Ankle
Voci	Shoulder blade	Qeteqete ni yava	Under instep
Domodomo ni liga	Wrist	Bukebuke ni yava	Heel
Qaqalo	Finger	Duru	Knee
Kuku	Nails	Voivoisiga	Front of shin
Kuku tau levu	Thumb	Domodomo ni yava	Bend of instep
Ai dusi	First finger	Domodomo ni yava	Instep

Where are you in pain? Ko sa rarawa e vei?
When did your illness begin? Sa tekivu ninaica na nomu mate?
Is your head in pain? Sa rarawa na ulumu?
Are your bowels open? Sa malumu na ketemu?
Are you costive? Sa kaukauwa na ketemu?
You must drink this. Mo sa gunuva sara oqo.
Drink this arrowroot. Gunuva na yabia oqo.
Have you the dysentery? Ko sa coka dra?
How long have you had this? Sa bogi vica vei iko oqo?
I have cut my hand. Au sa seleva na ligaqu.
A limb has fallen on me. Sa baleti au na taba ni kau.
I kicked my foot against a stone. Sa lauta na yavaqu na vatu.
My wife is very ill. Sa baca sara na watiqu.
Bind my arm with this. Vivia na ligaqu e na ka oqo.
Here is a pill for you to take. Sa dua na vua ni kau mo tiloma.
Come again in the morning. Lako tale mai e na mataka.
My arm is broken. Sa ramusu na ligaqu.

19.—RELATIONSHIP.

(I.) SOCIAL.

Father—Tama-qu.
Father, Grand—Tukai, tukaqu.
Father, Great Grand—Tukai vakarua.
Mother—Tinaqu.
Mother, Grand—Bui, buiqu.
Mother—Great Grand—Bui vakarua.
Husband—Watiqu.
Husband and wife—Veiwatini.
Father and child—Vaitamani.
Mother and child—Vitinani.
Parents and child—Veiluveni.
First-born (Male or Female)—Ulumatua.
Brother—Taci-qu. The elder is called by all the younger branches *tuakaqu*; and each calls the one older than himself *tuakaqu*. The elder calls all the younger *taciqu*; and the relationship of the whole is *veitacini*.
Sister—Taci-qu. The elder is called by all the younger branches, while they are young, *tuakaqu*; but when they arrive at youth, *gane–qu*. The elder call all the younger *taciqu*.
Grandchildren—The grandmother would call them *na makubuqu*; and the grandfather would call them *na maku*.
Cousins—Veitacini. But the children of brother and sister, being boys and girls, are *veidavolani*; and are considered *veiwatini*, or husband

and wife. Girl cousins call each other *veidauveni*; and boy cousins, *veitavaleni*. Boys and girls, cousins, will call each other *davalequ*. Cousins, children of brothers, are *veitacini*; but the boys of one brother and the girls of another brother are *veiganeni*, and it is tabu for them to speak to each other.

Uncle—Tamana levu, and tamana lailai. The children of a *younger* brother would call their uncle *tamaqu levu*, or great father; but the children of an *elder* brother would call their uncle *tamaqu lailai*, or little father, A sister's children would call their uncle *vugoqu*, and these only are *vasu* to the uncle. The children of an elder sister would call both uncle and aunt *gade*.

Aunt—Tinaqu levu and tinaqu lailai.

Father or Mother-in-Law—Vugoqu.

Brother-in-Law—A *man's* brother-in-law is *tavate*. A woman has no brothers-in-law.

Son or Daughter-in-Law—Vugoqu.

Sister-in-Law—A *woman's* sister-in-law is *dauve*, or *raiva*. A man has no sister-in-law.

Nephew—Luvequ lailai, a tagane. (*See* UNCLE.)

Niece—Luvequ lailai, alewa.

(2.) POLITICAL.

Tui—King, or principal chief. In times of peace he has unlimited power in his dominions. He has also lands peculiarly his own. Some are waste lands, and some are occupied by qali-kuro, or tenants at will.

Roko Tui—Is an official title and is the next person in authority to the king. His actual power will depend much upon his own ability. If he be a fool, he will have all the dirty work to do, and little of the honor or profits of his office—high sheriff. If he be an active and wise man, his honors and powers at home are equal to the king's, as he has much influence with the priests.

Vunivalu—This title belongs generally to a family distinct from the king's, although both are sometimes included in one, as at Bau. The duties and power of the office depend very much on the character of the ruling king. If he be all that his chiefs approve, then the *vunivalu* is a mere name; but if the king be disliked by the people, then this office is magnified by them, and the *vunivalu* becomes lord high admiral, &c.

Buli—Is to create, elect; but in some places it is a title of office, and the name of the place electing is generally added, as *Buli Nadi*, &c. They are generally elected fo r a year or two, and a great feast is prepared by the electors, and a large quantity of property by the elected.

Matanivanua—These were originally the lords of the soil. In some places they are little more than mere *mata*, or messengers to the chief places; but in chief towns they are men of influence in all political business. They are the principal speakers in all assemblies.

Taukei—The small land owners. Each family has its own lands; and for a chief to take family land for his own use, or to sell, is considered the greatest indignity that can be offered. The owners consider themselves *moku*, or killed, and generally leave the place.

Bati—Are the warriors, who are of several grades. In some kingdoms they are the ruling power, and no political movement can be made without their consent. They only prepare food on high occasions. In the Bau kingdom there are some inferior *bati*, who are a little more than *qali*.

Qali—Towns under tribute of food, mats, &c. Qali bring food almost daily to the chief's house. They are mere tenants at will.

Talatala—Is a person of some rank, or in whom the chief has confidence, who is sent to collect property or tribute.

Talaki—Is a menial. He is sent on trifling business; and has to endure *every sort of insult* from *everyone*, and especially from the *children* of the chief.

Mata—Is a political messenger. He is not appointed by his own people, but is elected by the place to which he is *mata*, and the appointment is ratified or rejected by his chiefs. While at home he represents the interests of his constituents; and when among them he represents the interests of his chiefs, and secures all the property he can for them. His dignity as *mata*, and theirs as *mata*, is raised or lowered according to the quantity of food or property he can secure for his chiefs. While he serves his constituents he is a *tolu* man, and can pass through their dominions although at war with the king's country. Some families are *mata* to the same place for generations.

(3.) FAMILY RIGHTS.

There seems to be three rights of interest in the lands—the chief, the family, and the individual. To secure peaceable possession, all lands should be bought by assembling all interests; viz.—the chiefs, and those who are *guards* of the family interests, or *matanivanua*.

No single individual should sell, except the chiefs who have *waste lands*.

(1.) Chiefs of *kingdoms* have lands that are their own; viz.—all lands and islands unoccupied, and some islands where the people are mere tenants at will—as *qali kuro*, and *qali kai tani*.

(2.) Chiefs of *districts* have also their own lands, as waste lands, and lands occupied by *qali kaisi* and *qali kai tani*.

(3.) Tribal chiefs. These seldom have any land of their own, except what they have in use; and have no power to sell family lands.

21.—A PAGE FOR THE NATURALIST AND BOTANIST TO FILL UP.

1. BIRDS. *Manu vuka.*

Batidamu
Beka, bat, vampire
Bekabeka, bat (small)
Belo, crane, heron
Bunikou
Dilu
Dilio, snipe
Dilio ni wasa
Druidelekula,
Naqiqi
Soqe, a large pigeon
Ganivatu
Kaka
Kawakawa, Bicitoka B.
Kitu, Maya, Tere, Qala,
Kikau, Kaisau
Lakaba, Kakabace
Lotui, Waituitui B.
Lawedua, boatswain
Manulevu, Tuivucilevu, eagle hawk
Micimieikula, kind of kula
Mo, kind of water hen
Saca
Seasea, Kerekereeai, kingfisher

Kula, paroquet
Kula votu, a small dove
Kilu
Tere
Lulu, owl
Kerekeresai
Kasaqa
Kacou
Kaisau
Manusa
Tokou
Tala
Toa, fowl
Manu levu, eagle
Taiseni, small kawk
Talaka vei rakula
Tomidenivuaka
Toqotoqo
Taca
Tecala
Teasea, kingfisher
Sawakila
Talesale
Qiqi
Qilu
Ga, duck
Pikoko, peacock
Pipi, turkey
Kusi, goose
Bici
Batikaciwa
Bune
Cou
Coki
Drei
Gogo
Gutulei
Toro, Tero
Vasuvasuaqiri
Yaragia
Yasaca, Saca B.,
Doli
Dreloa, sea bird
Malawe
Visakou, small crane
Gogosawa, sea bird
Gakiki
Lelcue
Takiwai
Solekura
Bicivukailagi
Kiko
Lawenivakatavu
Lelewai
Kalaba
Lewase
Se
Bulidamu
Kitou
Mamoa
Bulimarawa
Tabadamu
Kuluvotu
Qiliqili
Kolakola
Sigadrou
Riri
Vicio
Loke
Keteketecago
Betu
Manumanusole
Tute
Seava

2. Insects, Reptiles and Animals.

Asa, ass
Banuvi, or nuvi, caterpillar
Baca, bacaniqele, worm
Batibasaga, scorpion
Bativesi, kind of beetle
Bebe, butterfly
Beka, vampire bat
Boto, frog
Bukaroro, insect. Caicaiwai
Bulo-ma-kau, cattle
Butalawalawa,
Tinaniviritalawalawa } spider
Cikinovu, centipede
Dikedike, luminous insect
Dolu
Drekedrekevuata, firefly
Gasagasau, an echinus
  Qina, do with shorter spines
Gogo, cockroach
Gata, snake
Kadi
Kalavo, rat
Navanava, gnat
Ose, horse
Roqoroqo, insect
Sara, boar pig
Sarasara, worm or maggot
Sarasaradaliga, an insect
Sare, kind of lizard
Sarelevulevu, large ditto
Kosi, cat
Kokote, goat
Koli, dog
Kuma, a moth
Kutu, louse
Lago, fly
Lagotavuivui, fly or bee
Laimumu, kind of lizard
Laisare, ditto
Lairo, land crab
Lewasausau, the tarantula
Ligoligo, insect
Lo, Lolo, Qasikalolo, red ant
Lokoloko, insect in bad water
Lokata
Maka, locust of N.S.W.
Menasicinabelo, sea ear
Mimimata, ejects, a fœtid fluid at eyes
  of man
Moko, lizard
Nanu, mosquito
Nana, stinging gnat, sand fly
Vidividikoso,
  Vidiki, } hairy animal of sea
Vodre, grasshopper
Vodredraudrau, leaf insect
Vuaka, pig
Vunavuna, an insect
Vutovuto, sponge
Yane, a moth

THE FIJIAN LANGUAGE. 27

Soqolavuivui, hornet
Sipi, sheep
Sipi tagane, a ram
Sipi alewa, a ewe
Sugasuga, Kutukutu, an insect
Tatavukata
Taumuri,
  Vokai,   } chameleon
  Saumuri,
Ugavule, land lobster
Ulo, a maggot
Venu, an insect

Yavato, a maggot
Dakakulaci, amphibious snake
Bakui, hydra
Buikidi, a pig, a monster
Lokolokoniqio, } sea animal
  Kaliniqio,
Qiqisenimamawa, an animal
Qiqitabanidolu, sea animal
Veala, found on reefs
Vakasekeri, small qina
Lobilobiqalulu, an insect

3. Fish. *Ika*.

Kalia
Kanaci
Kara
Kulikuli
Kake
Koli ni wai
Kanailagi
Kawakawa
Kawago
Kurokoso
Kaikai
Kiuta
Ki
Tavuto
Tabacei
Toa
Ta
Tivitivi
Kaboa
Ai lati ni daveta
Regarega
Balagi
Bakewa
Balolo
Balara
Bonu
Babale
Babaloa
Bali
Dranimoli
Dadakulaca
Damu
Dabea
Delabulewa
Deke
Dekedeke
Drekeni
Dravua
Drauveisau
Qio
Qawaqawa
Qitawa
Lokaloka
Leuleu
Culacula
Cucu
Cumu
Curui
Corocoro

Babelo
Bobo
Bu
Reve
Baba
Vai
Vaida
Vai varovo
Vai vuka
Vonu
Vosevose
Vo
Veviwai
Malaivi
Magimagi
Matale
Mata ba
Molau,
Saku
Salala
Saqa
Sara
Soisoi
Se
Sabi
Via
Dokonui
Duna
Davilai
Uculuka
Uluburu
Ututoniika
Walu
Wiwi
Oma
Ose
Yatu
Yawa
Animasi
Noroi
Sabi
Sabu
Ciri
Dolokoto
Drevu
Tidaloko
Ogo
Veitakau

4. Shells. *Vivili*.

Katavatu,
Kuku
Kolakola
Kaikaso

Paikea
Bali
Bulikuka
Leivalekaleka

Kadawai
Kaitasiri
Kali ni qio
Kuka
Sici
Sisici
Sogasoga
Sigawale
Seniqeci
Sawawaqa
Kekewa
Vasua
Vavaba
Vula
Sagati
Vetuna
Civa
Cori
Cawaki
Cega
Qari
Qarivatu
Qaqa
Aikali
Lewerua
Lasawa
Lanilawa
Velyata
Vela
Waro
Tagane-ca
Bonubonu
Tabula
Sici, kei Ragata
Soubu

Toto
Bulileka
Bulibuli
Bousucu
Bakui
Bula
Burabura
Tivikea
Tovu
Tadruku
Tadrukutabua
Urau
Uga
Ugavuli
Drevula
Dio
Dri
Davui
Luila
Motodi
Mana
Yaro
Yaga
Yadrelevu
Gaca
Gera
Masinimataquli
Pipi
Tuivasa
Voce
Gada
Kailoa
Telei
Lairo
Sigawale

22.—WORDS NEEDING CARE WITH AI.

Ai balebale, meaning, tune
Ai binibini, heap
Ai biri, biriki, sticks to hold gates open
Ai bo, leaves strewed into the ley in which the natives dip their heads: yaqona strainer
Ai boi, scent [bread
Ai buli, the thing formed, as
Ai bulu, covering of a thing
Ai bulubulu, a grave
Ai bulukovu, knot of head dress
Ai butu, the fastening of thatch
Ai butiu, grass, sugar cane leaf
Ai caba, companion
Ai cabecabe, a steep place
Ai caca } broken pieces
Ai Kavokavoro
Ai cakacaka, manner of doing a thing
Ai kuri, an increase, addition

Ai bole, some interjection, phrases &c., so called, a proverb
Ai bono, a dam in watercourse
Ai boro, paint
Ai botani, a thing to stick on
Ai buku
Ai bulabula, yam sets, &c.
Ai daku, that which follows another
Ai daradaranitauoko, hole in tau through which tauoko passes
Ai davedave, channel for fluids, or their source
Ai davodavo } place to lie in
Ai kotokoto
Ai deredere, thing to wash in or clean with
Ai divi. a keepsake
Ai doini, wa or string to fasten crab's claws
Ai cina, a god

Ai calo, gouge of thing of hollow form
Ai caqe, cock's spurs. Laqe
Ai caraki, } it becomes them
Kedrai,
Ai cavacava, boundary, finishing end
Ai cavu, an ornament in vanua, a thing for which a place is eminent
Ai cegu, nonai cegu, your peace; appeals to one to save another
Ai cereki, anything eaten after
Ai ceu, a carving tool [full meal
Ai cibaciba, place at which departed spirits descend into bulu
Ai cili, a temporary house
Ai cobo, high precipitous rocks
Ai cobote, mouth of a cup, &c.
Ai vakacoa, food prepared for guests
Ai coco ni vale, grass on house floor Kenai coco, those strangled for chief to lie on when buried [food
Ai cokoti, leaves in basket for
Ai coka, tie beams of house
Ai coi, concomitant to food
Ai cokonaki, vakalolo fowl
Ai colacola, burden
Ai colanibuka, the shoulder
Ai cori, anything to which an animal is fastened, a snare
Ai covi, property to those who have fought and killed some one
Ai cuki, digging stick
Ai cula, needle [ingress, shirt
Ai curucuru, place of egress or
Ai dagi, eye water
Ai tau, eye water, B.
Ai dabedabe, a seat
Ai daini, } rope which holds
Ai tauoko } karikari to tau
Ai dolo, stick to swim on
Ai dovidovinikakana, the thumb
Ai dradra, second vine of yams
Ai drekedreke, burden carried as
Ai drodro, refuge [a pack
Ai drogadrogawale, fourth finger
Ai dudusi, forefinger
Ai gaga, hole out of which to drink from vessel [cloth
Ai ike, short stick for beating

Ai iloilo, looking glass, glass generally
Ai iri, a fan
Ai iro, a whisk of cocoanut husk
Ai kabakaba, ladder
Ai kadru, scraper
Ai kakalawa, a stile. Kalawa
Ai kaki, scraper (shell)
Ai kanakana, table
Ai kara, canoe pole. Doko B.
Ai kasa, companion
Ai kasi lairo, a string of land crabs. Wakai B.
Ai kasivi, spittle
Ai kasivibale, opening to spit out of [of canoe
Ai kaso, cross beams for deck
Ai kaso, children of inferior wife
Ai kasorara, plank in front of deck [kaso
Ai kasotu, middle and largest
Ai katalau, breakfast
Ai kau, heading of poem, part of meke
Ai kau vudi, bunch of bananas
Ai kaukau, burden
Ai kaukau, a gift
Ai kavilo, vudi leaf as a drink-
Ai kawakawa, bridge [ing cup
Ai kaweki, the tie of a karikari
Ai kedre, (in Vula Vou) the south wind generally blowing then
Ai kedru, a snore
Ai kelekele, heap
Ai kelekele, anchorage, anchor
Ai kere, interest, thing given for use of a thing begged
Ai vakatakilakila, a sign, &c.
Ai kosolaki, horizontal reed near top of house fence
Ai koti, scissors
Ai kuna, strangling rope
Ai labiniika, wrist
Ai labilabi, bundle of fish done up for c ˙ king
Ai lago, threshold, wooden rests
Ai lakolako, away or going
Ai lala, an omen generally of chief's death
Ai lalakai, native food-tray
Ai lati, a thing that conceals, curtain
Ai latu, stakes in fence of house

Ai latunaki, sinnet block
Ai lau, axe handle
Ai lawa, sinnet wrapping club
Ai lawaki, a cheater, &c.
Ai lekau, first fruits of breadfruit or first litter of pigs
Ai lelele, ferry canoe
Ai leqe, short wood in canoe
Ai leu, instrument for extracting thorns
Ai liko, bananas about a house
Ai lilili, clothes horse, &c., hammock
Ai liuliu, the first, one that precedes
Ai liumata, best property in front at Solevu.
Ai loba, backstay in canoe, yaqona strainer
Ai lokiloki, joint
Ai lokilokiniliga, elbow
Ai lokilokiniyava, knee
Ai lokoloko. pillow
Ai loloku, anything done out of respect for dead
Ai loloku ni laca, the rest, &c.
Ai loloma, a gift
Ai lumu, oil for body
Ai lutua, cook food for best heap
Ai macamaca ni coko, a scar
Ai madrali, offering
Ai masi, thing for scouring with
Ai matei, thorn fish-hook
Ai mei, a nurse
Ai milamila, a scratcher
Ai mocemoce, a bed
Ai mudremudre, an airy place
Ai muri, that which follows
Ai murimuri, the last, one that follows all the rest
Ai musunikola. a chisel
Ai naki, intention, purpose
Ai namata, mouth of basket to catch fish
Ai nasa, stick bent to strike by letting one end go
Ai nananu, thought
Ai nima, a baler [ing
Ai nokunoku, fish bent for cooking
Ai nono, place to lie on
Ai wolowolo B.,} bundle or
Ai oloolo, } faggot
Ai oviovi, a nest

Ai vaqa, provisions for journey or work [niu
Ai qali, bundle of nuts. Ai qali
Ai qalo, a thing to swim on
Ai qalovi, property to canoe before chief goes ashore when he goes for property
Ai qamu, pincers
Ai qaso, claws of animals
Ai qeu, stick for hairdressing
Ai qila, hooked stick for pulling down breadfruit
Ai qiliqili, small twists for platting sinnet
Ai qilo, end of tau in canoe
Ai qisa, vermilion face paint
Ai qiso, probing stick, ramrod
Ai qua, towel, &c.
Ai qumu, paint
Ai rabo, a sling
Ai rako, a grasp of the arms
Ai rara, a fireplace
Ai ravarava, a spade [of dead
Ai reguregu. presents to friends
Ai riri ni lolo, pot for boiling lolo
Ai roba. a striking
Ai rogele, a flag
Ai rogorogo, news, report
Ai roi, fly whisk
Ai roko, bow string
Ai roqo, small nursing mat
Ai roqonikena, breast fins of fish
Ai roro, a roost
Ai roroi, strengthening stick to karikari
Ai ruberube, a string for hanging anything up
Ai sa, a companion
Ai sagasaga, } tongs, a pair
Ai saga }
Ai sakalo, a great eater
Ai sala, head dress
Ai saluaki, a perfume
Ai samu, stick for beating cloth
Ai sarasaranidoko, part of canoe
Ai sasabai, shield
Ai sau, same as doko
Ai sau, retaliation, reward, punishment
Ai sausau, a reed stuck up to mark, &c.
Ai sauloki, ball of sinnet
Ai sausauvata, a stone set as a

tabu for food
Ai sauvola, a doko
Ai sava, a thing for washing with
Ai savenaki, slings to lift heavy things
Ai sele, knife
Ai selekoti, scissors
Ai seleiwau, sword
Ai sema, the joining
Ai semata, first fruits of vudi
Ai sere, ransom
Ai seru, a comb
Ai sese, a refuge
Ai sesetaki, the scattered refuges
Ai sevu, first fruits
Ai sevusevu ni yagona, first cup or branch
Sevu, often used as earnest, pledge and sample, of what is to follow
Ai sigana, offering to gods
Ai sikisiki, part of canoe
Ai silisili, a bath [yaqona
Ai sirovi, anything drunk after
Ai sivi, edged tool, spade
Ai sobesobe, a thing to hold on in order to go up or down
Ai sogo, shutter or door
Ai soko, the shell in which we shred a thing
Ai sole, winding sheet
Ai solesole, bundle
Ai solisoli, soli, a gift
Ai somai, a joint, also a piece added to a thing to lengthen it
Ai sominiwai, upper lip
Ai soqomi, bundle of spears given to warriors when they bole
Ai soqosoqo, an assembly
Ai sorisoriti, reeds on which thatch rests
Ai soro, an atonement
Ai soso, bunch of fruit or cluster
Ai sosomi, one in place of another
Ai sovasovanibenu, dunghill
Ai su, a basket
Ai sua, on oar ; also stick to take off husk of cocoanut
Ai suai, bathing apron, leaves
Ai sukui, upper joint of karikari
Ai tabani, anything added to complete a thing
Ai tabataba, laying hands on food (magiti), or expressing wish when magiti is presented
Ai tabatamata, generation
Ai tabayabaki, a season of year
Ai tabe, basket
Ai tabi, basket for food
Ai tabonaki, that which hides
Ai tadidi, pretended cause of complaint
Ai tadravu, offering to a god when yams all planted
Ai tagitagi, windpipe
Ai takataka, the source
Ai tala, property presented in return for (vakasobu) property
Ai talaki, a menial
Ai talatala, messenger
Ai tanituru, eaves of a house
Ai tarakete, membrane below
Ai taraki [ribs
Ai tasi, a razor
Ai tata, channel of water
Ai tata, chips, carpenter's work
Ai tata, the will or order of a chief
Ai tátá, paint brush, or rest for steer oar
Ai tatara, a thing to take hold of a thing with
Ai tau, eyewater, a friend, a branch thrown where one has seen a god
Ai taube, a necklace, &c.
Ai tauga, swinging shelf
Ai taukei, possessor
Ai taukukuniliga, (ni yava) finger or toe nail [nail
Ai taukukulailai, finger or toe
Ai taukukulevu, thumb or great toe nails
Ai tauraki, a menial
Ai tautau, property presented
Ai tautauri, handle or part by which held
Ai tauveti, ready to be plucked
Ai tauvutui, stones laid
Ai tavi, share or portion of work
Ai tavitaviraki, broom of cocoa-
Ai tavoi, towel [nut leaf
Ai tavu, charred stick
Ai tavucawa, steam bath
Ai tavue, stone used for anchor
Ai tavutubekau, part of turtle

Ai tei, yam set
Ai tekiteki, ornament for head
Ai tekivu, skein of sinnet
Ai tenumi, a fresh supply
Ai teteki, stones or logs to prevent earth falling into water
Ai tikotiko, property presented
Ai tikovaki, lady's maid
Ai tilotilo, throat
Ai tinitini, end
Ai tiniyara, train of chief's dress
Ai tiqa, a stick
Ai tivitivi, a hatchet
Ai tokoi, covering of house ridge
Ai tokani, a partizan
Ai tokatoka, (nearly synonymous with tutu and tikotiko), afterbirth
Ai toki, spoils of war
Ai toko, part of canoe
Ai toko, a prop
Ai tona, a piercer
Ai toqa, a saw or file
Ai toroi, a razor
Ai totoko, part of canoe
Ai tovo, nature, habit
Ai tubetube, handle
Ai tubutubu, ancestry
Ai tui, a basket
Ai tukituki, a hammer
Ai tukutuku, report
Ai tunudra, (magiti) food, after confinement
Ai turaki, an imitator
Ai tutu, a stand
Ai tutuna, shell for taking out the entrails of a fish
Ai tutunivu, part of canoe
Ai tutuvi, bed clothing
Ai tuvaki
Ai tuvalou, great quantity of cloth about a man at a solevu
Ai uaua, drumsticks
Ai ua, a stick for beating pudding
Ai ube, a covering
Ai ukuuku, glory
Ai ula, short-hand club
Ai usana, cargo
Ai vaci, shoulder blade
Ai vakacivo, a toast
Ai vakacoa, a custom
Ai vakada, yam reed
Ai vakadreudreu, men's bathing [dress

Ai vakamamaca, that given to the wrecked by those who save them
Ai vakaoqo, food for wife or mistress
Ai vakaravi (ni uli), a rest
Ai vakasigalevu, dinner
Ai vakasobu ni duru, men killed when a bure is kelivaki
Ai vakatoka, to name
Ai vakatoka, stick to keep cama up when drawn on shore
Ai vakatoka, anything petted
Ai vakavakarewa, the haulyards
Ai vakavakariba, trigger of gun
Ai vakavevede, a nest
Ai vakavotivoti ni bure, men killed when a bure is finished
Ai vakavotu, food taken before a woman's confinement
Ai vakavu, part of canoe
Ai vakana, yam head for seed
Ai vakayadra, breakfast
Ai vakayakavi, supper
Ai vako, a nail
Ai vakowiri, gimlet
Ai valavala, custom
Ai valu, war
Ai vana, mast
Ai vana, to shoot with a gun
Ai vaqa, food for voyage
Ai vaqali, small axe
Ai vaqaqa, a thing to make one qaqa
Ai varo, a file or saw
Ai varoro, a large or long saw
Ai vasa, pointed stick for game
Ai vasi, yam scraper, shell
Ai vatoto, sticks in cama
Ai vava, shoe
Ai vavaqumi, a war custom
Ai vavari, shell for scraping fish scales
Ai vavavi, cooking apparatus
Ai vavakoso, company
Ai vece, stick for breaking sticks
Ai vekaveka, the anus
Ai vesu, a bond fetter
Ai voce, oar, paddle
Ai vodovodo, a saddle
Ai vola, book
Ai voli, the price
Ai vorati, part of canoe

Ai vorosai, ribs (synonymous with waqawaqa)
Ai votuvota, a portion
Ai vuasagale, necklace of whales' teeth
Ai vuaviri, a basket
Ai vuavua, part of canoe
Ai vukeulu, killing some of a victorious army who have taken a town
Ai vukevuke, assistant
Ai vura, the stick with eye for thatching
Ai vuti, leaves used for yaqona
Ai vutu, dalo pestle
Ai vutuniwea, first fish caught in a wea
Ai wakai, string of land crabs
Ai waki, an ingredient
Ai wali, an ointment
Ai walui, a kai or scraper
Ai waro, a stick
Ai wase, food after yaqona
Ai yabo, person forbidden from touching food because he assisted in burying.
Ai yaca, grindstone
Ai yacoyaco, a thing come to pass
Ai yadrayadra, a club, spear
Ai yalayala, boundary
Ai yali, a spoon to stir with
Ai yaragi, arms, spears, &c.
Ai yaralaso, part of canoe
Ai yatu, a row (as—Ai yatu duru), a row of posts
Ai yau, property
Ai yawa, bunch, cluster of some fruits
Ai yaya, furniture, goods, chattels
Ai vakatukuwalu, a certain rope on a canoe
Ai tata, an axe or chopper or cleaver

23.—A SHORT VOCABULARY.

Abandoned, given up, sa biu
Abbreviate, vakalekalekataka
Able to do, sa cakava rawa
Abusive language, vosa ca
Accident, tawa nakiti
Accurate, dodonu sara
Ache, rarawa
Acknowledge, tukuna
Active, dauyavala
Add, kuria
Addition, ai kuri
Adrift, sa ciri
Afloat, sa nawa
Afraid, sa rere
Aged, sa qase
Agree in mind, me lomavata
Alive sa bula
All, kecega
Aloud, vakadomoilevu
Altogether, vata
Anger, cudru
To appoint (men), lesia ; (a time), lokuca
Army, ai valu
Ashamed, madua
Ashore, e vanua
Ask, taroga
Asleep, moce
Assist, vukea
Astern, kimuri
Attention, vakarorogo
To awake, vakayadrata
Awning, ai vakaruru
Axe, matau
Ballast, ai vakabibi ni waqa
Bamboo, bitu
Barter, veivoli
Bathe, sili
Beach, matasawa
To begin, vakatekivuna
Bend a sail, cokota na laca
Blast of wind, civocivo
Brace up, sila mai
To brush (sweep), taviraka
Bung, ai sogo ni saqa
Bunghole, a gusu ni saqa
Burnt, sa kama
Bury, buluta
Busy, ogaoga
Cable, ai noka ni waqa
Call, kacikaci
Cannot, sega ni rawata
To catch, taura
Certain, sa kila ne kena dina
Chain, sinucode
Chart, ai vola ni vanua

Choose, digitaka
To chop, taya
Civil in speech, dauvosa vinaka
Clean, savasava
To climb, kabata
To close or shut up, sogota
Covetous, Yalokocokoco
Cough, vu
To count, wilika
Crack, kaca
Crew (of a vessel), lewe ni waqa
Current, drodro, kui
Curtain (mosquito), taunamu
Cut (with a knife), seleva
Daily, e na veisiga
To dawn, sa kida na mataka
Deceit, veivakaisini
To decoy, temaka
To deliberate, bosea
To deny, cakitaka
Desirous. via *before a verb, as* via lako, desire to go
Destruction, rusa
Detach or separate, wasea
To detest, cata
Diarrhœa, coka
Discharge a cargo, me yau nai usana ki vanua
To disentangle, sereka
To disguise, vakalecalecavitaka
Dishonorable, vakaisi
Disobedient, talaidredre
Distance, yawa
Distinct (of sight), rairai vinaka
To distribute, vota
To disturb, yakayavalata
To dive, nunu
Diver, daununu
To do, cakava, kitaka
Done, sa caka oti
Dress, ai sulu
Easy (of work), rawarawa
Eatable, laukana
To ebb, sa voka na ua
Echo, a yaloyalo ni domoda
Edge, batina
To educate, vakavulica
Eel, duna
Emetic, a wai me lua kina
To endure, vosota
Enemy, meca
To enrage, vakacudruya
To enter, curu

Envy, vuvu
Equity, valavala dodonu
To err, cala
To escape, drobula
To escort, lako kaya
Etiquette, valavala vakaturaga
Everlasting, tawa oti
Every, kecega
To exaggerate, vakalevutaka
Excuse, ulubale
Expeditious, kusakusa
Expensive, sa levu na kenai voli
To explain, vakamacalataka
Explanation, ai balebale
To extinguish, bokoca
To faint, ciba
Faithful, dina
To fall, bale, lutu
False, lasu
Fat, uro
To fathom, katuma
Fear, rere, domobula
Feast, solevu, or magiti
Feel, yamoca
Feign sickness, mate lawaki
Figure-head, matakau
File, ai varo
Flag, kuila
Flint, qiwa
To float, nawa
To flog, vakanakuitataka
To fold, lobia
To follow, muria
Forbid, vakatatabuya
To force, vakasauraratakaa
Forcibly, vakaukauwa
To forget, guilecava
To forgive, lomana ga
Fortunate, daumaka
To foster, susuga
Foulmouthed, gusugusuca
Found, kune
To free, sereka
Frequently, wasoma
Fresh water, wai dranu
To fulfil, vakayacora
Full, sinai
To fumigate, kuvuya
Funeral, veibulu
To furl, vivia
Gale. cagikaukauwa
Gently, vakamalua
Giddy, matabuto

Gift, ka ni loloma
Girdle, ai vau ni toloda
To give, solia
Glad, marau
Glue, drega
To go, lako, bau
God, Kalou
Good, vinaka
To govern, lewa
Governor, turaga ni lewa
Grease, uro
Grindstone, ai yaca ni matau
To guard, vakatawa
Guest, vulagi
To guide (lead), tubera
Half-way, veimama ni sala
To halloo, kaci, kaila
To halve, wasea rua
Hammer, ai tukituki
Handle, (take hold of), taura
To hang, rubeca
Harbour (bay), toba
To harpoon, suaka
To hate, cata
To have, rawata
To haul, dre
Hazy, kabukabu
To hear, rogoca
To hearken, vakarogoca
Hearsay, talanoa walega
Heavy, bibi
Hidden, vuni
To hit, lauta
Hoe, ai kadrudadru
Hogstye, bai ni vuaka
Horizon, vu ni lagi
Humility, yalomalumalumu
To hurt (wound), lauta
Hypocrisy, veivakaisini
Idle, vucesa
To ignite, waqa mai
Ill-natured, yaloca
Immovable, sega ni yavala rawa
Impassable, sega ni lakovi rawa
Impertinent, vosa levu
To implicate, beitaka
To implore, kerea
Improper, tawa kilikili
Impudence, viavialevu
Incorrigible, sega ni vinaka rawa
Infectious, daudewa
To injure, vakacacana
Inland, lekutu, colo

Innocent, tawa kila (or not know)
Insensible (benumbed), nu
Inside, ad. eloma, n. loma, -na
Instantaneously, vakasauri
Intelligent, lomavuku
To intend, nakita
To intercede, sorovaka
To intercept, latia
Into, ki, kiloma
Invisible, tawa raici rawa
Irreligious, tawa lotu dina
Irresistible, tawa tarovi rawa
Irresolute, lomalomarua
Island, yanuyanu
Itch, karokaro, milamila
Jamb (verb), qaqia, kata
Joke, veiwali
To join, vauca vata, semata; cause to meet, utura
Joy, reki, marau
To jump, rika, lade
To justify, vakadonuya
Keel, takele
Keen (of edge), gata
Keep, taura, tiko; preserve, maroroya, karona
Keg, saqa
Key, ai dola
To kick, caqeta
Kidney, ivi
To kill, vakamatea
Knot (in rope), buku; in wood, suku, -na
Ladder, ai kabakaba
To lade, yau ki waqa nai usana
Lame in the knee, lokiloki; gera, lame in the hip
To lance, ciliva
Landing, matasawa
Lantern, ai vakaruru ni cina
Lard, uro ni vuaka
Late, taubera
To laugh, dredre
Leaf, drau, na
Leak, vakawai, lu
To lean, vakararavi
Length, kena balavu
Leprous, vukavuka
To lessen, vakalailaitaka
Lie, lasu, cori
Life, bula
Light (not heavy), mamada
Light (very), lacena

Light (not dark), rarama
Lightning, livaliva
To like, vinakata
Lime, lase
Loose (not firm), yavala
Lost, yali, takali
Loudly, vakadomoilevu
To love, lomana
To make, cakava, kitaka; make nets, tei lawa; make mats, tali ibi, make a fish fence, vola ba; make a canoe, ta waqa; make a feast, caka magiti; make a walk, cara sala; make a sail, cula laca; make an oven, caka lovo; make good, vakayacora.

N.B.— *When to make, in English, is followed by an Adjective, as,* to make long, *it may generally be turned into Fijian by prefixing* vaka; *and postfixing a termination to the corresponding Adjective; thus :*— Vakabalavutaka, to make long. *Thus also :*

To make bad, vakacacana
To make angry, vakacudruya
Many (of things), levu
Many (of men), lewe levu
Medicine, wai ni mate
To melt, vakawaicalataka
Midway, veiyawaki
Mine, } noqu; of food, qau; of
My   } drink, mequ
To mislead, vakacala
To miss (or mistake), cala kina
Moderately, vakamalua
Moist, kolumaca, suasua
Month, moon, vula
More, levu cake; there is some left, sa vo
Morning, mataka
Must, he must do it, e dodonu vua
Nail, ai vako   [me cakava
Naked, luvawale
Name, yacana
Narrow, qiqo, rabailailai
Navigable, sokoti rawa
Near, voleka
New, vou
News, ai rogo, ai tukutuku
Night, bogi
No, not, segai

To nod, (assent), deguvacu
To nod (with sleep), sosovu
No, there is none, sa segai
Nonsense, vosa vakalialia
Now, oqo
Oakum, ai bulu; to caulk, saubulu
Obey, talairawarawa
Ocean, wasa liwa
Oil, waiwai
Old, qase
Ooze, titiri, lu
To open, dolava
Orange, lecau
Origin, vu
Overgrown (with weeds), tubua
Oyster, dio, civa
Pack, ai solesole
To pack, solea
Padlock, ivi qaqa
Paid, sa voli oti
Pain, rarawa, mosi, toto
Paint, ai boro
Parcel, ai daba
Part, tikina
To patch, botani
Path, sala
Patience, dauvosota
Payment, ai voli, ai sau
Pearl, mataniciva
Pelt, virika
People, lewe ni vanua
Perfume, boi
Perplexed, taqaya
Perseverance, gumatua tiko
To pick (up), tomika
To pick (choose), digitaka
Pigeon, ruve
To pile, binia
Pincers, ai qamu
To place, virikoto
Plane, kai
Plank, papa
To point with the finger, dusia
Pot-hook, ai ruberubenikuro
To pour (in a small stream), livia
To pour (in a large stream), sova
Prawn, ura
Prayer, masu
Preach, vunau
Precipice, bati ni savu; when fall of water, bati ni savu; when no water, bati kali

THE FIJIAN LANGUAGE.

To prefer, vinakata cake
Presence (in the presence of), e na mata ni
Present (to be), sa tiko eke
To preserve, karona
To press, tabaka
Pressed down, bikai
To pretend, vakalasulasuya
To promise, yalata, yalataka
Pronounce, cavuta
To prop, tokona
Prow, kumi ni waqa
To pursue, cici muria
To pash, biliga
Quarrel, veileti
Quarrelsome, dauveivala
To quench, bokoca, suia
To question, taroga
Raft, waqa bilibili
To rain, sa tau na uca
Raw, droka
Recent, sega ni dede
Reef, cakau
Reef (sunken), buna [yamotu
Reef (small detached), namotu,
To reef (sail), musulaca
To refuse, bese
To remove (one's residence), tiko
To remove (for health), sese; (further off) toro yani, sudra yani
To repair, cakava tale me vinaka
To plant, talaca
To rest, vakacegu
Rinse (a cup), konekone
Rinse (the mouth), kubukubu
Ripe, dreu
To rob, butakoco
Room (there is room), sa lalaga
Rope, dali [ga
Rotten, vuca, rusa
To run, cici
Sabbath, siga tabu
To sail, soko
Sailor, kai wai
Salt, n. masima; a. tuituina
To scald, malabutata
To scorch, coroga
To scour, masia
To scrape, karia
Shallow, vodea, matia
Sheltered, vakaruru
To shift (of wind), voli, suka
Shot, gasau ni manumanu

Skin, koli, -na
Sky, lomalagi
To slacken, sereka
To slack (the sheet), sorova
To slacken (halyards), tukuca
To slap, tavia
Slippery, dravidravia
Slow, bera
Smoke, kubou
To snatch, kovea
Sour, wiwi
To span, cagava
Spark, lidi ni buka
To splice, semata
Sponge, vutovuto
Stamp, buturaka
Stand, wavu, tu
Star, kalokalo
Stove (for fire), miqa
Straight, dodonu
Strait, qiqo, rabailailai
To strand, kasa
Stranger, vulagi
Stride, kalawaca
To strike, yavita
To suit, lasa kaya
Sunrise (at), ni sa cabe na siga
Sunset (at), ni sa dromu na siga
Surf, se
Surprised, kidacala
To surround, vakavolivolita
To suspect, vakabakaya
Swamp, vucilevu
Sweat, buno
To sweep, tataviraka
Sweet, kamikamica
To swim, qalo
To tack (of a ship), rova
To tack (of a canoe), cava
Tail, bui-na
Tame, lasa, manoa
Tangled, tao
To thatch, ulata, tibika
Thick (of a board), vavaku
Thick (of liquids), sosoko
Thin (of solids), mamare
Thin (of fluids), waicala
Thing, ka
Thirst, viagunu
Thunder, kurukuru
To tire, oca
Tortoise, turtle, vonu
To tow, tuivutona

Toy, ka ni vakatalo
Track, we-na
Trial, veivakatovolei
Truth, dina
To turn, vuki
To twist, tobea
Umbrella, ai viu
To unbend, (a sail), tauluvataka
Unclean, qeleqelea
Uncultivated, lekutu
Union (of mind), loma vata
Unmoor, cavui kelekele
Up, cake
Upon, dela-na
To vindicate, vakadonuya
To vomit, lua
To wade, vuto
To wait, waraka

To warn, vakasalataka
To wash, sava
To watch, vakatawa
Water, wai
Wave, ua, biau
Weak, malumalumu
Weapons, ai yaragi
To weed, vutia na co
Well (of water), mataniwai
Where, evei
Wherefore, e na vuku ni cava
Whip, kuita
Whirlwind, covulaca
To whistle, kalu
Why, meicavai
Wick, wa ni cina
To win, tauca na cere
To wonder, kurabui.

www.ingramcontent.com/pod-product-compliance
Lightning Source LLC
LaVergne TN
LVHW051206080426
835508LV00021B/2842